TOUGH CALL

A Little Book On Making Big Decisions

MATT POPOVITS

ISBN: 0692746447
ISBN-13: 978-0692746448

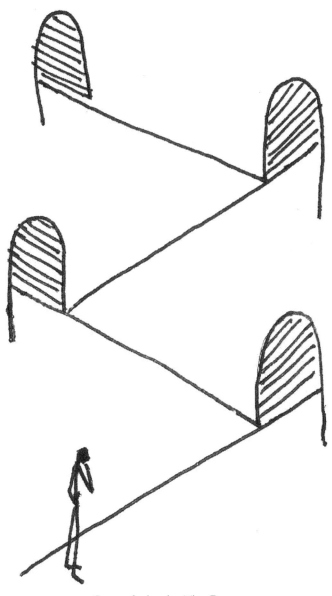

Cover design by Tim Bauer
www.timbauerdesign.com

FOR LISA

The best call I've ever made.

CONTENTS

INTRODUCTION

Welcome to life. It's full of tough calls and scary decisions.

Think about it: there are wedding proposals to ponder, college applications to submit, career moves to make, and the classic conundrum, whether or not to pay extra for guacamole when ordering a burrito. We desperately want to avoid making a fatal mistake. After all, history is littered with cautionary tales of men and women who, in hindsight, really screwed up.

No one wants to be like Dick Rowe, the executive at Decca Records who in 1962 passed on the audition tape of a new band saying, "Guitar groups just aren't hot anymore." That group was The Beatles. That decision cost him millions.

What about the myriad of publishers that said, "No thanks" to inking a deal with J.K. Rowling as she shopped the story of a young wizard named Harry Potter? You can bet they regret that decision. It's now the greatest selling book series of all time.

History buffs will point to events like the sinking of the Titanic, where Captain Ed Smith and his crew horrifically underestimated the difficulty of steering around an iceberg. That bad decision led to the tragic death of 1503 people and, sadly, to the fame of Leonardo DiCaprio.

And then there's Napoleon's invasion of Russia. Sure, he had the largest army ever assembled with some 600,000 soldiers. But Russia had two weapons that Napoleon failed to take seriously: head lice and a harsh winter. He retreated home to France having lost hundreds of thousands of men. Bad decision.

Knowing how poorly things could go, some people find themselves facing life's decisions with a deep and almost paralyzing fear of future regret. Those that are able to tackle the decision before them tend do so in one of three ways. There are instinctual decision makers, emotional decision makers, and the hyper-rational decision maker. Reading that list, chances are that you immediately know which of the three "styles" best describes you. The instinctual decision maker goes with her "gut." Without much pondering she knows what she wants to do and dives in, determined to figure things out as she plows forward. The emotional decision maker tends toward what "feels right." He reaches out for the option that conjures up the most positive sensation. Lastly, the hyper-rational decision maker aims for the most logical decision—the choice that rises to the top after he's done his research, weighed the pros and cons, and consulted the experts.

But consider this: whether you're an instinctual, emotional, or rational decision maker, how should a person of faith face a big decision? Is the follower of Jesus expected to approach life's tough calls and scary decisions just like anyone else or does the Christian faith offer a framework for facing decisions that minimizes fear, maximizes peace, and anchors our hope in something greater than our gut, our emotions, and our ability to do a Google search for the insight of others? I believe the answer to that question is "yes." And that's what this little book is all about.

ONE

THE POWER OF PERSPECTIVE

"If you look the right way, you can see that the whole world is a garden." - Frances Hodgson Burnett, *The Secret Garden*

Every year my family and I head out on vacation. We pile in the car or plop onto a plane and head out to some theme park in Florida, to a home we've rented on the coast with friends, or to stay with my in-laws in the middle of Michigan. Believe it or not, staying with the in-laws is a favorite option of mine for two reasons. One, it is significantly cheaper, as in free. And two, it requires far less parenting by me and my wife. We can let the kids go a bit wild with grandma and grandpa while mom and dad kick into neutral.

But even vacation is filled with "big" decisions. Should we sleep in really late or only super late? Should we eat a snack before we eat lunch or should we stop and eat a snack after dinner but before dessert? These are the things we are faced with while vacationing.

On a recent vacation we took the kids to a local bakery for breakfast. I told them that they could choose any donut they desired. I thought it was a simple ask from me, their generous and fun-loving dad. But no. Asking a 9-year-old girl with a serious sugar addiction which donut she wanted for breakfast is like asking her which puppy to save from a fire. She wanted them all and the fact that saying "yes" to sprinkles would mean saying "no" custard (we're talking donuts, not puppies) left her in tears. "I want them all," she said to me.

A HUMBLE PERSPECTIVE

The thing about decisions is that the one in front of us always seems huge, no matter what it is, whether it's choosing a donut or making a move in our career. But the reality is that while you and I will make countless decisions about important things in life, we will make far fewer truly critical decisions in life. One of the first things we must do is put our lives and our decisions--especially our really big ones--into perspective.

The thing about decisions is that the one in front of us always seems huge.

Reflect on these words from James:

> Come now, you who say, "Today or tomorrow we will
> go into such and such a town and spend a year there and
> trade and make a profit"— yet you do not know what
> tomorrow will bring. What is your life? For you are a
> mist that appears for a little time and then vanishes.
> Instead you ought to say, "If the Lord wills, we will live
> and do this or that." As it is, you boast in your
> arrogance. All such boasting is evil. (James 4:13-16)

James' point is that you and I have far less control over our
lives than we like to assume. And while that might, at first
blush, sound negative it's actually a very freeing truth. People
of faith are invited by the scriptures to have a humble view of
themselves. Yes, we have decisions to make. But we are
assuming way too much when we act as if a certain decision
will necessarily be the pivot point of our life, the fulcrum on
which our success or failure, our happiness or sadness will rest.
When we think that way we inch dangerously close to
assuming the job of God himself, who alone is charged with
ensuring that the arc of our lives lands in a place of peace and
joy. And, I would argue, a big part of the fear and anxiety we
feel when facing a decision can be attributed to pressure we've
placed on ourselves through assuming a level of sovereign

responsibility that our psyches simply can't bear.

The truth is that very often the small and easily overlooked decisions we make have as much, if not more, of an impact as the tough calls we spend weeks wringing our hands over. Take a moment and reflect on the truly life-changing events of your life. How many of them were the direct result of a big, gut-wrenching decision that you made? And how many were the result of split-second, seemingly random things that were largely out of your control?

You registered for an uninteresting college course simply because it fulfilled a requirement that you didn't set and allowed you to sleep in a little longer on Tuesday mornings. And on the first day of class you met your future husband.

Your dad changed lanes at the wrong time, an accident occurred, and the story of your life was forever altered.

You saw a sign in a store window as you walked down a street, decided to stop in, and a pair of shoes were purchased that later sparked a conversation at a party that led to you getting a new job.

Small decisions. Simple choices. Life-altering impact.

YOU ARE NOT IN THIS ALONE

Now, please understand, I am not fighting for a fatalist view of the world. I am not arguing that our decisions don't matter and that all of life is either completely random or pre-programmed.

Not at all. What I am saying, and what the scriptures teach, is that there are other forces at work in our lives. We are not the only ones steering the ship. The biggest force in your life is not chance or luck or even your own will and wisdom. The biggest force is the sovereign, all-powerful, hand of God. Your Heavenly Father has promised to guide the pieces of this puzzle called life into their proper place and to corral the random, risky, mundane and monumental moments of life toward his ultimate and good will.

The biggest force in your life is the sovereign, all-powerful, hand of God.

Step back and take in a new and peace-giving perspective. Look around and see that you are small and God is big, that you are limited in your ability to control the outcomes of life but that God is limitless in his love for you and able to usher all things toward his will. Take a deep breath and realize that the pressure is off.

In the face of a really tough call your first task is actually quite simple and incredibly freeing: to believe and confess that God, and not you, is in control. I know that what you are facing feels huge. But pretend, for a moment, that it's just a donut. Pick one. Enjoy it. And know that the God who worked through the baker to make it and through your dad to buy it is right now looking over your whole life and guiding it.

QUESTIONS TO CONSIDER:

What is it about this tough call that makes it feel so massive?
List briefly the things that you feel are at stake in this decision.

Can you name a decision from your past that at the time
loomed large but, in hindsight, was not quite as make-or-break
as it seemed?

TWO

EXAMINE YOUR HEART

"Most men would rather deny a hard truth than face it."
- George R.R. Martin, *A Game of Thrones*

Not long ago I was having a conversation with a friend. She was facing a big decision about her career with a deadline looming for a decision. She was offered a new and exciting opportunity and the future employer needed to know the very next day whether or not she'd be joining the team. The pressure of having to decide whether or not to leave a job she really liked for a role that she *might* really love was causing some major anxiety.

We downed several cups of coffee together as we listed pros and cons of the current job and of the one she was being offered. With every item we added to the lists I could see the muscles tightening in her shoulders and her breathing became increasingly shallow. She was really struggling. I stopped the process, placed my hand over the napkin, by now covered in hard-to-read scribbles of pros and cons, and I asked a question. "What are you afraid of?" It was clear to me that the source of her anxiety was a belief that the stakes of this decision were incredibly high, that should she make the "wrong" decision something bad would happen. So I wanted to know what that bad thing was. What was she afraid of?

What are you afraid of?

My friend looked me in the eyes and sat silently, slowly nodding her head in agreement, wordlessly acknowledging that this question was, in fact, at the heart of her anxiety. She thought for a moment, agreeing there must be some scary scenario she was desperately trying to avoid. "I don't know," she eventually shared. "I know I'm afraid of something. I just don't know what it is."

ANXIOUS AND INSECURE

I really appreciate how honest the Christian faith forces us to be. When we read or hear God's Word it opens us up like a skilled surgeon and it reveals who we truly are, and all of the brokenness we keep just below the surface. One of the many things we learn is that we are born deeply insecure. We are born disconnected, unmoored from a calming and clarifying relationship with God and with a heart in constant rebellion against his leadership. As a result we are quickly and easily convinced that we are on our own. We are tossed back and forth by the troubles of life, uncertain, anxious and ultimately afraid.

We are quickly and easily convinced that we are on our own.

We are afraid of missing out on a great opportunity. We live in fear of being rejected by the people whose opinions matter most. We are afraid that even if they do accept us, once they get a good look at us, they'll proclaim us to be unworthy. We feel like imposters, faking our way through all of the things we claim to be confident of and worried that at some point someone will burst into the room, point their finger at us and say, "Ah ha! I knew it!" We are afraid of making a stupid mistake and having to pay a steep price.

I find that an increasing number of people are living in fear of simply being normal. They're afraid of the idea of living an ordinary life. In a world where we, thanks to social media, are bombarded with the highlight reel of everyone else's "amazing existence" many are afraid of not being interesting enough. Have you considered that it's okay to be normal? God still loves you, and you are still fully accepted into his family of mercy through the work of Jesus Christ, if you decide to avoid the tyrannical pressure of trying to be interesting. If you choose to live a life where you love your family, where you are faithful at your job and kind to your neighbors, you are just as beloved in the eyes of God as your friend from high school who is designing her own clothing line, vacationing in Africa among orphans, and who drinks everything out of Pinterest-perfect Mason jars. Besides, there is an ironic struggle that many of us, who desperately run after the interesting life, are discovering: we spend so much time curating an exciting life that we often forget to enjoy the actual moment and be present with the people around us. In our effort to show the world that we are making the most of life we are, in fact, missing out on life.

As we approach a tough call it's important to recognize the presence of fear, not simply because it's a good exercise in honesty but because our fears and insecurities have a powerful influence over us in the face of a big decision. Our fears love to lie to us, convincing us that our situation is completely unique and that no one has ever faced a crossroads quite like this before. Our fears tell us that no one around us really "gets" what we are facing and that none of the standard wisdom or traditional rules apply to us. And it's when we buy into those kinds of lies that our anxieties ramp up and that the potential for doing something truly foolish actually increases.

CONFESS YOUR FEARS

When I was a kid my brothers and I would spend hours wandering in the woods behind our country home. Hiking along the muddy edge of our favorite creek we'd often stop to turn over an old, fallen tree or lift up some big rock tucked deep in the dirt. We did this because underneath every log in the woods was a world of gross, of slugs and bugs and ugly things--the kinds of things that 9 year-old boys love to dare their brothers to eat.

Christians have a strange belief when it comes to fear. We are not big on victoriously overcoming our fears or therapeutically analyzing our fears. Although both of those things are fine, if you can pull them off. Christians believe that fears are meant first and foremost to be confessed. As we walk through life we are called to flip over every log, notice the nastiness underneath, and confess it to God, acknowledging its existence and handing it to him.

Christians believe that fears are meant first and foremost to be confessed.

Psalm 139 captures this idea perfectly:

Search me, God, and know my heart! Try me and know my thoughts! See if there be any grievous way in me, and lead me in the way everlasting! (Psalm 139:23-24)

King David, who undoubtedly faced some incredibly heavy decisions, wrote this song in which he invited God to rummage through the recesses of his heart and mind. He invited God to uncover all that was broken and to lead him down a path dictated not by personal rebellion and unrealistic fear but down a divine path, filled with God's peace-giving and unchanging promise of mercy.

What are you afraid of? If you were to turn over the log, to make David's prayer your own and ask God to examine your heart and to investigate the dark corners of your big decision, what would he find? What unfortunate outcome are you desperately trying to avoid? What worry is really driving you? That's a scary question to ask. Some of us simply don't want to confront the truth of our fears. But do you know what's even more frightening to me? The prospect of getting to the end of my life and realizing that I made big decisions based not on the promises of my Heavenly Father but on the unfounded fears and the trivial concerns of my broken heart and my fragile ego.

I know it might not be an easy exercise, examining your heart and confessing your fears to God. But I promise that it's worth it. On the other side of confessing our fears is something deeply comforting and truly helpful: love. At the heart of the Christian faith is the belief that confession of sin, which includes our fears, is met with the life-changing love of God. Every single time.

DEEPLY LOVED

God relentlessly loves you--underside of the rock and all. He is undeterred in his love by the slugs, bugs, and nastiness that clings to you. He is not put off by your problems. He loves you knowing full well the fears in your heart and the freakiness of your soul. Sure, the awful things you reveal must be repented of, but what is repentance but turning over the rock and calling upon the love of God in the face of what you see? God's message to you, every time you hand him the confession of who you really are, is that he loves you. He loves you not because of the potential he sees in you, or because he trusts you to make the right decision. He loves you because his son Jesus Christ has won forgiveness for you and has earned for you an unqualified acceptance into his grace and mercy. He loves you because Jesus Christ faced every fear on your behalf, was crushed under their weight as a way to drain the evils of this world of their damning venom and to pay the price for your constant rebellion against God's leadership. He loves you because Jesus Christ then rose from the dead, showed his power over every single human fear, and declared to the universe that all those who have faith in him have no reason to cower in terror but are fully and forever covered in the mercy and grace that he has earned. And now, every time you confess your fears to him, he quiets you and calms you with this promise: in Christ, you are loved. And that love, as it hits your heart, affects you. It changes you. The New Testament puts it like this:

> There is no fear in love, but perfect love casts out fear. For fear has to do with punishment, and whoever fears has not been perfected in love. (1 John 4:18)

FREED BY LOVE

John's words are great. Knowing that we have divine acceptance is a freeing reality. If you are loved by God then every fear that is driving you or paralyzing you is ultimately rendered illegitimate. Why? Because the one who holds the past and the future in his hands loves you! The one at the top of the "food-chain of approval" accepts you. He calls you beloved because of Christ. What then do you really have to fear? I mean, *really*?

Such love frees us to do something more with our tough calls than to simply avoid pain or look out for our own interests. Knowing we are completely loved frees us to see our decisions through the lens of sacrificial love. Secure in the eyes of God, we are free to leverage our lives and our big decisions to bless someone other than ourselves. We are freed to make not just personally beneficial decisions but beautiful ones. We are free to consider doing something that may cost us deeply but benefit someone else tremendously. And when we enter into that kind of territory with our tough calls we are reflecting, in wonderful ways, the love we have received and we are swimming in the rare and restful waters of real freedom.

But it all begins when you pause, for a moment, from scrawling your pros and cons and you start examining your own heart. As a friend, allow me to place a hand on your ink-stained Starbucks napkin and ask you a question...

"What are you afraid of?"

QUESTIONS TO CONSIDER:

What do you imagine to be the worst possible outcome of this decision, and what about that potential reality frightens you so much?

Who is at the top of the "food-chain-of-approval" for you? How might your desire to please this person be influencing how you see this tough call?

THREE

INVITE THE WISDOM OF OTHERS

"Without good direction, people lose their way;
the more wise counsel you follow, the better your chances."
- King Solomon, Proverbs 11:14 (*The Message*)

Who is the wisest person that you know? As you consider that question, keep in mind that there is a difference between being wise and being smart. It's hard to explain but the difference is significant. Your friend who writes codes for a living is smart. Your cousin who runs circles around you in math, and who has never once needed to count using her fingers to help solve some simple equation, is smart. But wisdom is different.

Smart is all about knowing certain facts and mastering difficult skills. Wisdom is another brand of insight altogether. It's less data-driven and more people-driven. It's less task-focused and more life-focused. Just because you understand how my computer works, can do my taxes for me, or are currently working to engineer a cancer-curing superdrug doesn't necessarily mean you're also the right person to go to for advice after a bad breakup.

To be wise is to have an inherent understanding of how human beings operate, of the aims we all have, the evils we embrace, and the struggles we share. You might hear a Christian say that a wise person has a keen perception of God's natural law. They have a fundamental grasp of the overarching values and the guiding principles that the Creator has ingrained into this universe.

ROBERT AND LOUETTA

Two of the wisest people I've ever met were an elderly couple, Robert and Louetta. They were residents at a nursing home I volunteered at while in graduate school. Robert and Louetta were the same age, 102, and had been married for 80 years. Each week when I arrived they, along with a handful of their nursing home neighbors, would wheel themselves over to the community room to take part in a short Bible study that I-- armed with my sharpest insights from my most recent classes-- had very smartly prepared. Week after week the group would listen closely, ask a few polite questions, and then express their gratitude.

Early on in the cycle of our weekly meetings I got to know Robert and Louetta and became fascinated by their longevity in marriage. I was touched by the genuine affection they displayed for each other after so many years together. At the time, I had been married for all of 15 seconds and was hungry for helpful insights on how to build a love that could last a lifetime. Each study ended with the amen of a closing prayer, upon which I would turn to my 102-year-old friends and pepper them with questions about marriage and family. One afternoon I asked them this, "What is the secret? If you had to boil it down to one truth, one piece of advice for married couples what would it be?" Louetta chimed in quickly. "Forgive each other." Robert however took his time. He thought for a few moments then, leaning in, placed his 102-year-old hand on my arm and looked me straight in the eyes confident that he was about to give me a life lesson of immeasurable value. "Son," he said. "Know when to shut the hell up." The other residents gathered around the table in the community room nodded their heads in vigorous agreement. "Sometimes the best thing to do is to stop the fighting, say, 'I love you,' and then close your mouth." Louetta seconded her husband's advice with a hearty "Amen." As a man who has now been happily married for many years I can tell you that Robert was spot on. Robert and Louetta were wise.

WELCOME WISDOM

Until now the conversation about how to make a tough call has focused largely on internal things: changing your perspective and confessing your fears. Having done that you're ready to begin tackling the issue itself, to begin approaching a decision and determining what to do. The first practical step to take is to invite the wisdom of others; to scan the horizon of your life, take note of some of the wise men and women that God has put around you, and give them a chance to speak into the decision at hand.

Time and again, the Christian scriptures underscore the importance of seeking wise counsel. Consider, as an example, just two verses from the book of Proverbs:

Without counsel plans fail, but with many advisers they succeed. (Proverbs 15:22)

Whoever isolates himself seeks his own desire; he breaks out against all sound judgment. (Proverbs 18:1)

The Christian scriptures paint a very low picture of humanity. Yes, human beings are the crown of God's creation and yes, he loves us with an inexhaustible passion and showers us in a ludicrous amount of mercy, won for us through the perfect life and sacrificial death of Jesus Christ. Yet, there is no getting around the fact that we are still deeply flawed, to state things mildly. This is especially evident when it comes to making tough calls and big decisions. As seriously screwed up people we tend to gravitate toward the choice that is easy, not necessarily the one that is right. When no one else is looking we let our corrupt hearts overly influence the logic in our brains and the work of our hands. We do what we want, not what's required. Not only that, but left alone our logic is handicapped by our own limited experiences and we are relegated to the resources of our small, individual brains.

As seriously screwed up people we tend to gravitate toward the choice that is easy, not necessarily the one that is right.

God urges those facing tough calls to invite the wisdom of others because in the gathered community of family and friends we find two things that messed up people, facing a major crossroads, desperately need: accountability and insight. It's tougher to tap out of a tough decision and take the low road when people that you love and respect are watching. With their eyes on you and with their questions welcomed you'll feel the pull to carefully consider your options and determine what's best. Likewise, after inviting the wisdom of others you'll have a far deeper reservoir of knowledge to draw from and more life experience to lean on.

DESIGNED TO DEPEND

God is not a fan of you living your life in isolation. In the Old Testament book of Genesis we hear about the origin of all things. God handcrafted all that we see, including the first human, Adam. He placed this man in the Garden of Eden with work to do and decisions to make. And even before this same creation was corrupted by Adam's rebellion God looked at this single, solitary individual and he said, "It's not good for man to be alone." (Genesis 2:18) And so God made Eve.

Think about that. Before the world was corrupted by rebellion, flooding it with all of our present problems, before humanity's heart turned sour, God designed and commanded Adam, our ancestor, to manage life and make decisions *with Eve*. Meaning, if you insist on facing life's tough calls on your own you are rebelling against God's design for human existence. Like it or not, God has wired this world to work in a certain way. No man, no woman, is an island. God insists on depositing knowledge through networks of people, distributing courage through connection and community, and dissipating your doubts through the encouragement of others.

If you insist on facing life's tough calls on your own you are rebelling against God's design for human existence.

FINDING THE WISE ONES

At this point you might be thinking the following:

> *"Okay I get it. We are not intended to face these tough calls alone. We need to seek out the wisdom of others. In doing so we benefit not only from their collective insight but from the added accountability. But where do I find these wise people? How do I know who to ask? And when I do find them what in the world do I say? 'Hi! I'm Matt. I'm crippled with fear in the face of big decisions. Can you help me figure a few things out? And while you're at it will you tie my shoes and cut the peanut butter and jelly sandwich my mom made me for lunch into perfect squares? Please!?'"*

I understand your angst, but seeking out the wisdom of others is actually quite simple. First, when it comes to "who" to seek out I suggest that you look for someone who knows you, who shares your worldview, and whose own choices in life you respect. That's really it. Seek out someone who knows enough about you to ascertain if a certain option in front of you might be out of character for you or at odds with what they know to be your aims in life. Seek out someone who shares your view of the world and your deepest values. If you're a Christian it's best to seek the wisdom of someone who shares your faith and who can give you wisdom and encouragement along the lines of the truths you share and the hope you both have. Lastly, look for someone whose own choices in life--on the whole or in a particular arena related to your tough call--impress you. Often this will be someone who is older than you and who is now enjoying the fruit of solid decision-making.

As you reflect on those three criteria, who comes to mind?

AN AGENDA-FREE ASK

As you approach someone for advice try your best to do so without an agenda, other than to get their honest input on your decision. We tend to approach others with a desired outcome in mind. Rather than seeking actual, unbiased insight on what we should do, what we are really seeking is affirmation or permission for what we want to do.

You know how this works. You approach a friend for advice and as you begin to describe "Option A" your smile widens and your eyes light up faster than a hippie with glaucoma. (Think about it.) But when you get to "Option B" your shoulders slump, your smile fades, and those listening start asking if your dog just died. You lay out the various options but your body language and the tone of your voice make it clear that you've got a favorite. And, since most people simply want to be liked, they'll tell you exactly what you want to hear. So, as you approach them do your best to either hide your bias or, better yet, be upfront about it and ask them to challenge it.

MY OWN TOUGH CALL

One of the toughest calls of my life came a few years ago. I was presented with the opportunity to start a church in New York City, something that had been on my mind for a long time. But doing so would require leaving a ministry in Texas that I deeply loved and which was, by most standards, wildly successful. The church was large and growing. I was surrounded by a team of talented friends who made the tiring work of ministry truly fun. Most importantly my family was thriving. Despite the many reasons to stay in Texas I felt stuck as I faced the decision, unsure of what to do.

Seeing that I was struggling, a friend reached out with some advice. "You need other voices in your life right now, Matt. Ask some other people to share their wisdom." She was right. I made a few phone calls and gathered a group of wise counselors, 6 people in all. It was a diverse group, for sure. But they each had at least two things in common. First, they each knew me and loved my family. And second, they each shared my view of the world and my core belief system. That was it. I met with the group as a whole and later, took the time to speak with each one individually. I laid out the facts, described my options, pointed out my biases and confessed my fears. They asked lots of questions. Really great questions.

A few days after the conversations had ended I reached out to each of my wise counselors and I asked them: "Should I stay or should I go?" To a person they each said, "It seems crazy, but we think you should go." Their clear and unified counsel wasn't the only factor in our decision. But it was a big one. We moved to New York City three months later.

Staring down a tough call can feel terribly lonely. But just because you feel alone doesn't mean you actually have to do it alone. Chances are high that you're surrounded by some very wise people who are ready to speak into your scary decision right now. Find them, and prepare to be surprised, not just at what they'll say, but at who they will be. Your wise counsel could be your successful friend or that professor from college that you've kept in touch with. Give them a call. But Wisdom could also be enjoying dinner at 3 in the afternoon, followed by an exciting game of gin rummy, before falling asleep next to her husband of 80 years at the nursing home down the street. You never know.

Look around. Seek them out. And invite them in.

Questions to Consider:

How would you describe your reliance upon others in the face of a big decision? Are you tempted to go it alone or do you find comfort in the idea of other counselors?

Think of two people who know you well, who share your worldview, and whose own life choices you respect. Have you invited them to speak into this decision? If not, what's stopping you?

FOUR

INTERROGATE THE OPPORTUNITIES

"Judge a man by his questions rather than by his answers."

- Voltaire

My dad is a car guy. I have vivid memories of being 8 years old, my dad buying me and my brothers ice cream and then ushering us down row after row of classic automobiles at one of the Saturday night car shows so common in the summertime in the middle of Michigan. I remember him pausing to chat with each car's proud owner, typically a retired husband and wife team donning matching t-shirts and relaxed in lawn chairs next to their special ride. "Mr. and Mrs. Car Show" were always happy to answer my dad's questions and eager to shoo away little boys attempting to lay their ice-cream-coated fingers on the quarter panel of their 1964 Chevrolet

Corvette Stingray.

My dad loves cars. My dad knows cars. He can fix just about anything on a car. I, on the other hand? I can drive cars. That's it. And if you ask my wife, even that statement is a stretch. One time, after driving to dinner and pulling into the parking lot, I glanced over at my wife and she had a strange look on her face. It was a mix of relief, of slowly waning fear, and of gratitude for the gift of life--think of a schoolchild in 1940's Britain peering out from under her desk after the air raid siren goes quiet. After I had shifted the car into park she grabbed my hand and said, "I love being your wife. But I hate being your passenger." So yeah, I'm not a car guy.

Whenever it's time to buy a car I try to take my dad along with me, even as an adult. He simply knows what to look for-- better yet he knows what questions to ask. I'm the kind of guy that could easily purchase a car based on sticker price and paint color alone. But my dad comes to the dealership locked and loaded with great questions and a keen eye. I've watched him scan the rubber window trim of a used car looking for faint specks of paint, a sure sign he says that a car has been in an accident and taken to a less-than-reputable body shop. He's been there to feed me detailed questions about warranty coverage to ask a salesman. He's revved many an engine for me, ready to discern knocks and rattles that I would never notice, and to encourage me to consider walking away or making an offer. When I buy a car I try to bring my dad because he helps me to investigate the potential purchase and interrogate the opportunity. And afterward I'm always well-equipped to make a smart decision.

QUESTIONS ARE YOUR FRIEND

As you face your tough call you too need to ask a lot of questions. You may think the "price" is right and the "paint color" is perfect but it's your job to dig deeper. You need to interrogate the opportunity in front of you. In the previous chapter we discussed the importance of surrounding yourself with wise people. That crew of insightful friends and family will help you discern the right questions to ask and to sort through the answers as they emerge. The wise people around you can *equip you* with good questions to ask, just like my dad at the dealership. But the questions remain *yours to ask,* just as the car--the answers and the outcomes--will be yours to live with.

It's your job to dig deeper. You need to interrogate the opportunity in front of you.

Sadly many people, even when equipped with really good questions, refuse to interrogate the opportunities in front of them. Perhaps they already have a preferred course of action lodged in their hearts and are afraid that new information will force them off course. Or maybe they simply fear complicating an already stressful process with more data to consider.

Whatever the reason, they opt out of a critical part of the decision-making process and choose to live in ignorance. They roll the dice and choose the car simply because it's their favorite color and they can afford the monthly payment, only to be surprised when otherwise avoidable issues and foreseeable problems confront them shortly down the road.

TWO QUESTIONS

At a basic, superficial level there are two questions you should be using to interrogate the opportunity in front of you. First, "Is it possible?" Second, "Will it be enjoyable?"

"Is it possible," as in do you actually have the ability to pull it off? Do you have the skills to do the new job, the income to honestly afford the new home, the strength to forge a network of friends in that new and far away city? Sometimes we run towards an opportunity without ever taking a serious look at our abilities. We fall in love with the idea of something without ever doing an inventory of our skills or assets, without honestly questioning if we have what it takes to accomplish that task or succeed in that new scenario.

Likewise, will you enjoy this particular opportunity should you take it? You may find it strange that you should ask whether or not you would enjoy a certain decision. After all, who in their right mind would consider an opportunity they know they would dislike? You'd be surprised. It's not so much that we choose things we know we would hate, it's that we often fail to consider what actually brings us joy. Often as we look honestly at an opportunity or a particular decision we will discover that although it might be a good thing in theory that it's not the right thing for you. Discerning that takes honest and practical questions about what it will take for you to be deeply satisfied, about what is necessary for you to have joy.

Will you be satisfied with not just having the new title but doing the new work, day after day, that comes with the promotion?

Does this guy bring out the best in you? Do you like who you are when you're with him?

Are you really okay with the fact that this girl you're dating doesn't share your faith?

Will this purchase truly enhance your quality of life or will you be looking for something else once the shine wears off?

As you begin to actually live with this decision will you still enjoy this decision?

Some will find that these two questions alone are a sufficient interrogation. But as I said earlier they are somewhat superficial. People of faith are encouraged to dig even deeper.

A QUESTION OF FAITHFULNESS

The Christian scriptures speak to us like a loving father, leaning in and whispering in our ear as we wander the used car lot of life. They tell us to not only ask if something is possible and if it will be truly enjoyable. Above all they encourage us to ask this deeper and more critical question: "Is it faithful?"

Yes, you've already invited the wisdom of friends and family to influence your tough call. But there comes a point where you must take into account all of the outside information you've received and personally wrestle with the integrity of the options in front of you. It's a journey toward deep and brutal honesty that only you can take. To question the integrity, the faithfulness of an opportunity is to hold it next to your deepest beliefs, your core values, your highest aims and wonder aloud, "Do these things line up?"

To question the faithfulness of an opportunity is to hold it next to your core values and wonder aloud, "Do these things line up?"

If your parents were anything like mine then they were fond of saying things like, "Just because you can doesn't mean you should." Such sayings were mom and dad's way to get you to look beyond the superficial factors in a given scenario and to question its faithfulness, to question whether or not it aligns with the values they instilled and the person you want to become. That invitation still stands. Although now it's not coming from your mom. As Christians would say, it's coming from your Heavenly Father. And an amazing thing about the pursuit of faithfulness, in the face of a big decision, is that God explicitly promises to give us the insight and wisdom required to discern a faithful path.

> If any of you lacks wisdom, let him ask God, who gives generously to all without reproach, and it will be given him. But let him ask in faith, with no doubting, for the one who doubts is like a wave of the sea that is driven and tossed by the wind. (James 1:5-6)

The Bible couldn't be clearer on this point. If you ask God, full of faith in his good disposition toward you through the work of Jesus Christ, for help in determining a faithful path forward then he will grant it. Period. And it makes sense. Parents love to tell their children what to do. What good parent, when asked by his or her child for insight and perspective, would ever hold back? God is no different. If you ask him to make clear the morality of a given choice or the integrity of your logic in light of his law and in comparison to his commands he will always answer that prayer. You may not like what he says. But he will answer. So at the risk of stating the obvious you might want to pause right now, say a simple prayer, and take him up on that offer.

Interrogating the opportunity in front of you by examining its faithfulness can take on a lot of forms. But a solid line of questioning could sound something like this:

"In light of what I know to be right and wrong, honorable and questionable, obedient and rebellious, where does this opportunity fall?"

"When I consider the goals I have for my life, the goods I'm called to manage, the people I'm tasked to love, and the God I want to honor, is this choice a step in the right direction or a diversion I should avoid?"

Chances are good that if you're asking deep questions like these the fog surrounding your big decision will begin to burn off. The creative rationalizations you've made to prop up a poor option will become evident. When you ask not just what is possible or what might be enjoyable but you also begin to ask what is faithful the contrast between good choices and bad choices, between smart choices and self-indulgent choices becomes sharper. The road ahead gets just a bit clearer.

YOU ARE NOT ALONE

Why wouldn't you ask deep questions about the tough call you're facing? Sure, you may very well feel ill-equipped to lead an investigation of the opportunities in front of you. You may be afraid of what you'll learn by digging under your desires and analyzing the integrity of your options. But remember, you don't have to head to the used car lot alone. You have access to a Heavenly Father who knows way more than you do. And if you ask him for help in looking under the hood he'll be there in a heartbeat, whispering all the right questions into your ear.

Questions to Consider:

As you face this tough call reflect on the options in front of you. Ask of each option the following questions: "Is it possible?" and "Will it be enjoyable?"

Having reflected on what you *can* do, shift the focus to what you *should* do. Wrestling with each option, and taking into consideration your core values, ask this question: "Is it faithful?"

FIVE

MAKE A MOVE

"You cannot swim for new horizons until you have courage to lose sight of the shore." - William Faulkner

"At some point you just have to jump."

Those were the words I shouted to my 5-year-old daughter. She had been standing at the outside of the pool, tiny toes curled around its edge, staring at the bright blue water for most of the afternoon. She wanted to dive in. She wanted to jump off of the edge. She wanted to land in the water and feel the rush of being pulled back to the surface by the Minnie Mouse floaters wrapped tight around her arms. But there she stood. Frozen in the summer sun.

There are moments as a parent, even as the parent of a kindergartener, where you sit back and wait. You've coached them up. You've hugged and assured them. You've even bribed them. "Dive in and we'll have ice cream for dinner!" But in the end diving into the water is still up to them. At some point the analysis has to end. The questions have to cease. The interrogation must come to a close. At some point you just have to make a move. You have to either jump into the water or walk away from the pool. Standing there, wondering and wrestling indefinitely, gets you nowhere and wastes a good afternoon in the sun.

EVENTUALLY IT'S TIME TO JUMP

It'd be nice if, after doing the hard work of assessing your tough call, the road ahead was clearly marked. Sure, sometimes it will be--the best decision will be plain to see. Other times, after all of your wrestling, it will still be a bit fuzzy and you'll feel deeply uncertain. It can also be the case that, after assessment, several options in front of you seem viable. Whatever the scenario they all have one thing in common. They all require you to act.

You'd like to be assured of success. But that's not possible. You'd like a guarantee on the front end that you've made the right decision. You'd love some sort of promise that you won't end up with water in your nose, freaking out, crying on your dad's shoulder and snot smeared all over your sun-kissed face. But guarantees of success aren't part of the deal.

You just have to jump. And that's when the real journey begins.

YOU MOVE, GOD GUIDES

I once had a friend say to me, "God is kind of like GPS. He does his best work once you start moving." Thus far we've talked exclusively about discerning the best decision in the face of your tough call. But that's only part of the journey, and a relatively small one at that. God does his best work, the bulk of his work, as he walks with you through the implications of your decision. That's what makes him, in the mind of my friend, a lot like the GPS that's in your car and on your phone. Setting the destination is hugely important. But God also has his sights set on challenging and encouraging you, on equipping and empowering you as you move forward. God doesn't move parked cars, so to speak. He guides, directs, and helps us as we choose a path and head down the road.

One of the more well-known and oft quoted verses in the Bible says this:

Your word is a lamp to my feet and a light to my path. (Psalm 119:105)

It's popular because of the incredible comfort it offers people of faith. God promises that through his word, through the

Christian Scriptures--specifically, in the promise of Jesus Christ--God will work in you and for you as you live out your decision. He will give you continued clarity and direction, illuminating your path.

Now, that doesn't mean that the road ahead, following your tough call, will be easy, with God giving you exact coordinates toward successful living. It just means that as you stay close to God's truth he will guide your steps. But it will still require a great deal of faith from you, along the way. Notice that the psalmist uses the imagery of a lamp--not the sun in the sky or a blazing bonfire but a lamp. Ancient lamps were small, often filled with olive oil and cupped in one hand. The flame was tiny and the light it made was meager. In the darkness of the ancient world it was enough to illuminate the next few steps. That's about it.

As a child I used to go camping in the summer with my family. As an adult however, I'm yet to camp. Let's just say that my wife, whom I deeply love, is not the outdoor type. She argues that it's uncomfortable and dangerous. According to my wife humans wrapped in sleeping bags are the soft tacos of the bear world. So no, we don't camp. But if, unlike my wife, you've enjoyed the thrill of sleeping outside then you've gotten a good sense of what it's like to walk with God after making your tough call. You get up in the middle of the night to use the bathroom. So you grab the flashlight and head out for a walk. With the help of the flashlight you can see. Kind of. You can focus it on the path in front of you or on objects around you, but it doesn't erase the darkness completely. It only shows you so much. Even though you have a light it's still, largely, a walk of faith.

> *Even though you have a light it's still, largely, a walk of faith.*

That's what it will be like as you move forward following your tough call. Even if you make the perfect decision the road ahead will still be a walk of faith, one of trust and dependence with God guiding every step of the way. The good news for people of faith is that he promises to walk with you, to equip you, and to use the journey to challenge you and change you. But no matter what, it's a journey that will require an immense amount of trust from you.

MOVING MAKES YOU READY

I've counseled lots of young, married couples who are looking forward to having children but express a fear that they're simply not ready. They don't have enough wisdom, enough money, or enough courage to raise a kid on their own. I have to lovingly inform them that there's no such thing as being ready for parenthood, as a married couple. But rather having the child itself is what makes you ready.

In many ways the same is true with your tough call. If

you're not just waiting for the decision to become clear but for the road ahead to become plainly marked and faith free, guaranteeing your success or previewing every possible pitfall then you will wait forever. That's not how things work. That's not how God works. Your task is to make the best decision you can, based on the information you have in front of you and to trust God the rest of the way. He will guide you. Moving makes you ready.

Your job is to dive into the water or walk back into the house and to trust that either your mom will meet you with a fresh towel or your dad will wrap his arms around you in the pool and teach you how to swim. But standing still, all afternoon, with Minnie Mouse floaters wrapped tight around your arms is not an option. It's the waste of a beautiful day.

It's time to take a leap or take a walk.

It's time to make a move.

QUESTIONS TO CONSIDER:

If you were to make a decision on your tough call today--if you were to choose a direction and move forward now--what would your first step involve?

Consider what you'll need with you on the road ahead. Who are the people and what are the practices that, when part of your life, leave you feeling equipped and encouraged?

SIX

REST IN GOD'S GOODNESS

"When you've seen beyond yourself, then you may find, peace of mind is waiting there." - George Harrison

Once the tough call is made it's time to rest. I'm not talking about rest as in "check out of life, curl up on the couch, and take a nap" but more of an emotional and spiritual state of relaxation and ease. It's true that your big decision may have invited a new season of work into your life. You may now have a wedding to plan, a new job to prepare for, a home to sell, or a degree to pursue. There may be no time for naps. But for the person of faith there is an invitation for your heart and mind, even in a very busy season, to be at ease.

THE PEACE OF GOD

The person of faith is called in the Christian scriptures to rest in the goodness of God, a goodness that has been proven to you not in the guarantee of a certain outcome, but in the life, death, and resurrection of Jesus Christ. The apostle Paul, a first century pastor and church planter, once wrote to encourage a nervous and anxiety-ridden group of Christians. He said this:

> Do not be anxious about anything, but in everything by prayer and supplication with thanksgiving let your requests be made known to God. And the peace of God, which surpasses all understanding, will guard your hearts and your minds in Christ Jesus. (Philippians 4:6-7)

I appreciate Paul's words. He directs the person of faith, facing uncertainty, to take their concerns about the road ahead to God and to receive, in trade, the peace that comes from knowing all that's guaranteed to us through the finished work of Jesus Christ. When most people reflect on the benefits that come from having faith in Christ their minds jump to visions of eternity, of pearly gates, puffy clouds, and a reunion with lost loved ones. Having faith in Christ gets us so much more than a ticket to Heaven. Don't get me wrong, eternity is a big part of it. It's just not all of it. The life, death, and resurrection of Christ have major, peace-inducing implications for the life you live today in the aftermath of your tough call.

Here's just a glimpse of what you can be confident of, because of Christ, following your big decision. You can rest assured that God will *realign you*, that he will *rescue you*, and that in the very end he will *resurrect you*. Let's take a look at each one.

GOD WILL REALIGN

One of the great promises of the Christian faith is that Jesus Christ, through his perfect life and sacrificial death, has earned you a place in God the Father's family. You have a seat at his table and he calls you daughter, he sees you as his son. His perfect life has served as a replacement for your wandering existence. His sacrificial death has paid for and pushed aside any animosity that once existed between you and God. Through the death and resurrection of Christ, God the Father looks at you and he doesn't see "sinner" or "failure" or anything else. He looks at you and all he sees is a member of his family. And since you're one of the family, God has promised to do for you what any good parent would do for their son or daughter as he watches them walk through life. He promises to step in, if you get way off course, and realign you.

You have a seat at God's table and he calls you daughter, he sees you as his son.

When I was a child I had a remote controlled car. It was the simple, inexpensive kind that only moved back and forth. The ones that allowed you to control the turns and to round

49

corners were a little too pricey for my parents. This meant that as you played with it, if the car got off course, there was no correcting it unless you paused the fun, ran to the car, picked it up and pointed it back in the right direction. God will do the same to you. If you get off track in this new endeavor he will run to intercede and work to set you straight. And you should expect some twists and turns in the road ahead.

Victor Hugo wrote in his classic *Les Miserables*, "The straight line, a respectable optical illusion which ruins many a man." In other words, things never go according to plan. But God will still be a good father, ready to intercede and point you forward. That helping hand may come in the form of wise friends and loving family stepping up and speaking truth to you. It may come in the form of a sermon on a Sunday morning--the kind where it seems like the preacher has been reading your text messages because he's illustrating your exact frustrations. It may come in the form of God's own Spirit, promised to you as one of his children, convicting you in your conscience and driving you to realignment. It may come in the form of an empathetic employer or a compassionate coworker who sees you struggling, or who notices a potential pitfall and reaches out to guide and correct.

GOD WILL RESCUE

You can be confident that along the way, as you walk forward in this decision, God will not only realign you but, if need be, he will rescue you. This is not to say that bad things won't happen. They will. The marriage you're entering could end in divorce. The money you're investing may dry up and disappear. You may find that this new job, despite really wanting it, really isn't a good fit for you. Bad things will happen. But God promises to rescue you, albeit in a particular way.

God doesn't often pull us from the clutches of problems but rescues us by redeeming our problems. He uses them to teach us lessons, to shape our character, to open our hearts and expand our minds. He uses our struggles to remind us of our frailty and to reveal to us our deep and constant need for his mercy--which he generously supplies. In this sense the problems and pitfalls you're bound to face have immense purpose and meaning. God will always be there to creatively work a story of grace in and through your moments of weakness and seasons of struggle. And for God, it's safe to say that getting a chance to offer you a real and vulnerable encounter with his love is a better ending, from his perspective, than if everything had gone perfectly in the first place.

God doesn't often pull us from the clutches of problems but rescues us by redeeming our problems.

He will rescue you in that he will often meet you in the depths of despair and lift your heart back to the beauty of his promises. As the fruit of your decisions dissolves into something sad or frustrating it's tempting to use it as a lens through which to view your entire life and even your relationship with God. We are quick to think, "I'm a failure and God has forgotten me." But in those moments, those who are close to God's word and connected to his people, will hear from him a reminder that nothing will ever separate them from his love. God refuses to judge us based on the outcome of our choices. No matter what kind of problem we find ourselves in God will never remove his loving hand or turn his back on us in disappointment. We often choose to see ourselves through the lens of our lowest points and as a result we second-guess everything we have. God however sees us through the lens of Jesus Christ and as a result promises to always give us what we need: his love.

GOD WILL RESURRECT

You can be confident that in the very end God, this God who has realigned and rescued you, will also resurrect you. For people of faith this is the pinnacle of all of God's promises.

Let's just imagine, for a moment, that the worst of all possible things happens: you make your tough call and it costs you everything. You choose a particular path and it blows up in your face. Sure God realigns you a few times along the way and rescues you from total despair, but in the very end things haven't gone to plan and you head to your deathbed with a deep sense of regret. Despite your best efforts and your fervent prayers you failed to sign The Beatles, you sunk the Titanic and got lice in Russia. You die wondering about what might have been and you use whatever energy is left in your failing body to kick yourself as you crawl into the grave.

That's really bad. But for people of faith that's not the end. Thank God.

Christians hold tight to a promise that one day Jesus, who now is seated at the right hand of God the Father, will return. And when he does he will resurrect every body that's been laying in the ground and reconnect it with its soul that's been resting in his presence. At that moment of resurrection, where we are made new, the entire universe--all of creation--will be re-created and restored. We will then live forever, in flesh and blood, in a new world, with none of its previous problems, for eternity.

It's a hard thing to wrap your mind around, impossible almost. But give it a try. It's worth the effort. Because if that promise is true then it means there will come a day when you and I will get a grand "do-over" so to speak, a fresh start and a new beginning in a better world. It will be a world filled with an overwhelming sense of God's presence, of his goodness and his glory, so near that it blocks out any view of the painful past and so bright that the memories of our most boneheaded, gut-wrenching, regrettable choices, burn away like the morning fog in the face of a glowing, rising sun. That's the promise of resurrection.

Yes, resurrection feels a bit far-fetched and is seemingly impossible to grasp. But it's going to happen. We can be sure of it. Not simply because the Christian scriptures say so, but because Christ himself has already risen from the dead. His resurrection is as much a fact of human history as anything else. Something happened 2,000 years ago in the outskirts of Jerusalem. It was something so mind-blowing, so fantastic that the echoes of it are still reverberating in our time. It was something so awe-inspiring that those who witnessed it instantly dedicated their lives to it. Something so pivotal that most of the world, to this day, measures time against it. 2,000 years ago Jesus Christ rose from the grave following a horrific death, a truly terrible and tragic turn of events. He rose from that tragedy, which saw him dead and defeated, glorified. And he promises the same to you. For those that have faith in him the worst may in fact happen, but a brand new day will come. Guaranteed.

BUSY HANDS, PEACEFUL HEART

Once you've made the decision it's time to rest, not to be lazy but to rest. It's time not only to set your hands to the tasks before you but also to set your heart and your mind at ease within you. You're his child. He's a good parent. Trust that as you move forward he will be there to guide your steps, to keep you close, and--in the very end--to raise you back up.

What do you have to worry about? God's got this under control.

QUESTIONS TO CONSIDER:

How do you feel about the fact that there will be twists and turns in the road ahead? Are you the type of person who cringes at the loss of control or are you at peace with the fact that so much of life is left to the hands and promises of God?

Can you think of a time in the past when God has corrected or realigned you? If so, how does that shape your view of the road ahead?

SEVEN

PRAY

"Prayer does not change God, but it changes the one who offers it." - Soren Kierkegaard

I once had the opportunity to chat with one of my favorite baseball players--and by chat I mean ask him one question in front of about 500 other fans. But still, I like to think we shared a moment.

A few months prior to our very brief interaction he had made one of the greatest plays of his career, in the World Series no less. In the bottom of the tenth inning, with two outs and two strikes--just one pitch away from losing the game and the series and going home empty-handed--he knocked a hit into right field to tie the score. They went on to win the game and eventually the championship. I asked him what it was like to stand in the batter's box knowing that millions of people were watching you, and that your split second decision would be the difference between going home a hero and hanging your head--on national television--in frustration and shame. His answer surprised me:

> "I prayed. I didn't pray that I would get a hit. I just prayed that I'd have a good at-bat, that I'd make good choices and leave the results up to God. That way, no matter what happened, I could round the bases or walk back to the dugout in peace."

His answer surprised me for two reasons. First, I was surprised to hear that he prayed at all. I probably shouldn't be so cynical. But I believe from my own experience, and from my conversations with others, that our instinct as human beings-- even those that consider themselves to be a person of faith--is to dive immediately into the work of "getting a hit." Confronted with a pivotal moment in life we launch directly into doing, strategizing, planning and executing with little--if any--time given to prayer. We immediately take the moment into our own hands and neglect the need to pause and put it all in God's hands.

Confronted with a pivotal moment in life we launch directly into doing with little--if any--

time given to prayer.

Second, I was surprised by the prayer itself. He didn't ask for a hit. A hit was what he wanted. A hit was what every fan watching nervously in the stands or pacing in front of their television was desperately hoping for. Most of us, when confronted with a pivotal moment in life, a critical decision in our career or a turning point in an important relationship are quick to say to God, "This is what I want! Please make it happen!" And on one hand there is nothing wrong with that. Like any good parent God wants his children to come to him, and to trust him with the desires of their hearts. And yet, my favorite ball player, in the biggest moment of his career, didn't ask for what he wanted. He simply asked for a good at-bat.

ALL-STAR WISDOM

I think there is real wisdom in this all-star's words. I think there is something instructive and useful for you, in his prayer. Firstly yes, you *should* pray. Rather than dive right in you should pause and pour out your heart to God. Don't worry about the beauty of your words just share your fears, articulate your hopes, and invite his help.

As a side note, if you're reading this and you're not a person of faith I'd encourage you not to immediately discount this part of the process. You may not consider yourself a believer, or be much for prayer, but consider this: what could it hurt? Either way you're facing a major moment in life. If you stop to pray and God turns out in the end to be some figment of the human imagination what have you lost? In fact you're probably *still* ahead of the game because the very act of prayer requires a bit of deep reflection and gives you the chance to verbalize what you're feeling. Any therapist--Christian or not-- will tell you that those two disciplines are beneficial to the human psyche. But if God does exist, if God is real, then you've got everything to gain. You will have invited the one who made the mountains and set the stars in place to be mindful of your pivotal moment. And if he does choose to hear you and to help you then you will be, without question, better off because of it.

But not only should you pray, asking God to grant you the desires of your heart. But you too should ask for a "good at-bat." Taking into consideration all that you've read it should be clear by now that the outcome of your tough call is ultimately out of your control. You can, and should, invite the wisdom of others. You must wrestle with the faithfulness of the options in front of you. You have to make a move and rest in the goodness of God to get you through it all. But you cannot pre-program the ending, like a coder in Silicon Valley who gets to design an app and create a world of her choosing to sell to our smartphones. As we've discussed, that's not your job. The wise and mature prayer is one that asks God not only for what you want, but in particular asks God to guide you, to help you with the things that are actually within your control. It's a prayer that asks God to assist you in the things that he's charged you alone to do.

Why would an all-star athlete choose not to pray for a hit in the biggest game of his life? Think about it. Typically, a great player will hit around .300 over the course of his career. That is, for every ten at-bats, you can count on him getting three hits. Or to think of it another way, part of being great is learning to deal with frustration and disappointment 70% of the time. He's learned early and often that getting exactly what he wants, whenever he steps up to the plate, just isn't possible. It isn't part of the plan. And so he adjusts. He decides that the goal can't simply be the hit he desires. It has to be approaching the opportunity to the best of his ability, being faithful with the elements of the moment that are in his control, and setting aside the things that are not. He can't control the fact that the opposing pitcher is at the top of his game on that particular day, or that the right fielder is about to make a highlight-reel catch at his expense. All he is responsible for is being faithful in that moment. And the same is true for you.

God has asked you to face this crossroads, as evident by the fact that, well, you're facing it. God has asked you to wrestle with what's in front of you and to take the best swing you can at the best pitch you see. That's your job. So ask him for discerning eyes. Ask him for a clear mind and a peace-filled heart. Ask him to help you trust the right people. Ask him to give you the guts to end the deliberations and make a move. Ask him to ease your anxiety and increase your confidence as you live out the implications of your tough call. Ask him to help you be responsible and faithful on the road ahead. That's it.

A PRIMER ON PRAYER

I realize that prayer is a subject that makes many people uncomfortable. Not because they are averse to it. They're uncomfortable because they feel ill-equipped for it. They worry about saying the wrong things or sounding stupid as they rattle off their requests to God. Do you remember the first time you heard the sound of your own voice played back to you? If you're like most your response was to say, with disgust, "Is that what I *really* sound like?" It seems like most people take that impression and apply it to how God must perceive their prayers. "How can he stand to listen to me? Let alone answer me? I sound like an idiot."

The proper Christian view of prayer is actually quite freeing for those who worry that their prayers sound foolish. The Christian scriptures teach that all prayer is "Trinitarian." That is, it involves all three persons of the one true God. Jesus himself instructs us, when we pray, to call out to our "Father."

It's an easy point to overlook, but if God is to be understood--according to Jesus himself--as a father this has deep and practical implications on how we should approach him. We should approach him knowing that he wants to hear from us and that he expects us to bring the concerns of a child. He expects us to be rambling a bit, to be worried about things that he already has figured out, and to be confident of his dad-strength. No child, with a good father, worries about how his words are perceived. He just jumps on his lap and starts talking.

Jesus himself, as the savior of the world, is the one who gives you the right, the privilege to approach God as your Father. John in his gospel, which details the life, death, and resurrection of Jesus, puts it like this:

"To all who believed, He gave the power to become children of God." (John 1:12)

Those whose hope, whose trust is not in their own life and abilities but in the life and the ability of Jesus Christ are welcomed by pure grace to God's table. We are, because of Jesus Christ, members of his family. This is why you'll often hear Christians conclude their prayers by saying, "In Jesus' name, amen." Saying so is a way to recognize, to confess, that through Jesus Christ you have the right to call God your father and to ask him anything you want.

This is an important point for those who doubt whether or not they can or should approach God in prayer. Perhaps you have a keen awareness of your flaws and failings and you assume that a holy God would want nothing to do with a mess like you. Or perhaps you simply think of God as you would any high-level leader; only those who have attained a certain status, who have the correct clearance and certain credentials have the ability to approach. Your resume needs a few more good works or great intentions added to it before you could dare to casually call upon God. This logic is understandable and pervasive. But it also happens to be wrong. At least in light of the Christian message.

At the heart of the Christian message is the proclamation--to any ear willing to listen--that God loves horrible and profoundly imperfect people. Why? Because that's the only kind of person that exists. And any effort to present yourself to God as good enough to be called his child or accomplished enough to bend his ear is futile and foolish. However, in Jesus Christ--God's own son--God the Father has made a way for you. Christians believe that while our imperfection is deeper than we want to admit God's love for humanity is bigger than we could ever comprehend. Out of love God sent his son Jesus Christ to live the perfect life you refuse to and are unable to. In his death on the cross Jesus Christ took the punishment for every evil and injustice perpetrated by you and done against you. And in his rise from the grave Jesus proved his work on your behalf sufficient and the power in his hands unmatched: he defeated death. And it's this work that earns the world the right to approach God as a Father, without fear. Christ has covered your corruption with his perfection. He's erased the potential of your punishment by nails piercing his own hands and feet. You are, in Christ, a daughter of the one true Father, a son of the almighty God. So talk to him. Jesus has given you every right to do so.

At the heart of the Christian message is the proclamation that God loves horrible and profoundly imperfect people. Why? That's the only kind of person that exists.

To top it off, Christians believe that our prayers are enhanced and empowered by God himself. God's Holy Spirit is promised to all those who believe in Christ and it serves as the fuel of sorts, in the engine of faith. Christian theology paints a beautifully lopsided picture of salvation. Not only does God the Father send his son to live, die and rise for you, but he sends his own Spirit to enable your beliefs and to empower your prayers. The Holy Spirit is said to be the one who stirs up the desire to pray, gives you the words to pray, and even works overtime on your behalf, pleading your case before God on those days where you really want to talk to God but are too exasperated or confused to put the words together.

For Christians prayer is Trinitarian. It is done to God the Father who loves us, in the name of Jesus who has earned a place in the family for us, and by the power of the Spirit who stirs within us and works behind the scenes for us. You might think that the prayers you offer sound goofy or self-indulgent. And maybe they are. But who cares? If what the Christian scriptures say is true then you have God's ear, you have full access, and your prayers have power. Don't let the sound of your own voice stop you from praying. It certainly doesn't stop God from listening and answering. You'd be foolish, as you face this tough call, not to rely upon such an incredible resource.

PERSISTENT IN PRAYER

You might be wondering why this chapter is at the end of the book rather than the beginning. A good case could be made that this discussion should take place first. After all, for a person of faith prayer should be one of the initial steps in the decision-making process not the last. Truth is, the reason this chapter is last is because I believe that prayer is not merely something you do at the outset of a tough call. But because it's an essential part of the process after you make that tough call.

Everything we've discussed up to this point happens prior to and at the moment of your big decision. But prayer, I would argue, is the one step, the one task, that remains with you as you live with your decision. Once you leap, the tough calls aren't over. In many ways they are just beginning. That relationship, the one you decided to commit to, is going to have complexities you need to navigate. That career you decided to pursue is going to challenge you and present character-building obstacles to you. The employee you chose to let go is going to have some questions for you. The business you decided to start is going to demand an incredible amount of time and energy from you. In order to live with this decision you will need a deep reservoir of strength to draw from. Where does that come from? To walk faithfully into the future the one "step" that stays is the need to relentlessly call upon God, who promises to care for you and be with you every step of the way. The reason this chapter is at the end is because prayer is the discipline that a wise decision-maker carries with her into the future.

NOT ALONE AND UNAFRAID

You're not alone in this. At least you don't have to be. You have the chance to surround yourself with a chorus of wise and supportive voices. You should do that. But more importantly you have the opportunity to face this and every other decision in life with the greatest of all allies attentive to your needs and listening to your wants. You'd be wise to take him up on the offer.

Go ahead, ask for it all to work out perfectly. But ask him also to help you approach the moment faithfully. And know that whether you round the bases as a hero or head to the dugout in disgust you are not the sum total of achievements. You are the object of God's affections. No matter how this tough call turns out your identity is secure. You can have peace. You are his. You are loved.

QUESTIONS TO CONSIDER:

What is your biggest obstacle when it comes to prayer? Is it a matter of making the time, overcoming fears, or trusting that you're actually being heard?

Consider your daily routine. Is there something that you do each day--a drive to work, a run on the treadmill--that could also be utilized as a regular time of prayer?

EPILOGUE

This tough call is just one of many, of countless decisions big and small that you will make from this moment forward. Some will play out perfectly. Others, not so much. And odds are that you read this book looking for some practical advice or spiritual insights on how to ensure that the decision you're about to make will result in something deeply satisfying if not downright amazing. I hope it helped.

But consider this. Maybe making the right decision isn't the point. Perhaps the greater purpose in this, and in every tough call you face, is not so much the outcome itself, but the way you approach each opportunity and the path you walk after each decision? What if this tough call--with all of its angst and uncertainty, with all of your fear of failure--is not about avoiding a certain outcome but, through the process itself, becoming a certain person?

In all of this your character will be forged. Your faith will be tested. To face and make a tough call is to ask deep questions, take big risks, and to pray passionate prayers. And through that process you can't help but walk away changed. And maybe who you are becoming is more important than where you're going and what you're avoiding. Maybe.

I'm a Christian and I'm a pastor. Those two points were, I'm sure, impossible to overlook as you read the previous pages. But as a Christian and a pastor, I have come to a belief that God is far less concerned about our lives turning out a certain way than he is about our hearts turning toward him.

We tend to live our lives consumed with things like our career trajectory, our relationship status, and our bank account. And these things matter. They really do. But, in God's grand scheme of things, they matter far less than knowing him, receiving grace from him, and being made into the image and likeness of his son, Jesus Christ. And as such while we tend to see our decisions as critical turning points on our way to a particular and glorious destination God tends to see them--and all of life--as tools he uses to forge us--often through great struggle--into different people. He uses life's decisions as a crucible of sorts, in which he breaks us open so that we might know our deep needs, perceive his great love, and learn some beautiful truths.

All that to say this: don't just focus on making the right

decision. Be aware that something--someone--else is at work. This book started by recognizing the fact that we all want to avoid epic and embarrassing failures. But keep in mind that you can steer around the iceberg and sign The Beatles and still miss the point of life. Pay attention to your heart. Don't just ask, "What's the right thing for me to do?" But ask also, "What might God be doing in me?" That question will help you zero in on the task that truly matters, which is not just being a success, but becoming a new creation, aware of your deep deficiencies and trusting completely in God's mercy.

ABOUT THE AUTHOR

Matt Popovits was born in Flint, Michigan but now lives and works in New York City where he serves as Pastor of Our Saviour New York (OSNY), a family of parishes in Manhattan and Queens, working together to serve the city.

Matt is also the host of *The Spiritual Howcast* on YouTube, which offers insightful yet simple answers to the spiritual questions of skeptical people, and a regular speaker at events and conferences around the world.

Matt and his high school sweetheart Lisa proudly live in the borough of Queens with their two children.

For more information: mattpopovits.com

Made in the
USA
Columbia, SC